ST. ISABELLA CATHOLIC SCHOOL LIBRARY
CALGARY, ALBERTA

Holidays

Stewart Gardiner

Holidays are special days.

We have holidays to remember people from the past.
We have holidays to remember events from the past.

★ Martin Luther King, Jr.

In January we have a holiday.
It is called Martin Luther King Day.

On this day people remember
Martin Luther King, Jr.
He worked for equality for all people
in our country.

★ **Abraham Lincoln**

In February we have a holiday.
It is called Presidents' Day.

White House

George Washington

On this day people remember America's presidents. America's presidents helped build our country.

Vietnam Veterans Memorial

In May we have a holiday.
It is called Memorial Day.

On this day people remember
the people that have died for our country.

In July we have a holiday.

It is called Independence Day.

On this day people remember
the birthday of our country.
On this holiday there are picnics
and fireworks.

In October we have a holiday.
It is called Columbus Day.

On this day people remember Christopher Columbus's first voyage to America.

In November we have a holiday.
It is called Thanksgiving.

On this day people remember
the pilgrims who settled here.
On this holiday people gather together
for a special meal and give thanks.

What is your favorite holiday?